By R. D. Rosen,
Harry Prichett
& Rob Battles

with Sad Truths
by James Friedman

bad
president

Workman Publishing,
New York

Library of Congress Cataloging-in-Publication Data is
available.

ISBN-13: 978-0-7611-4620-9
ISBN-10: 0-7611-4620-2

Design by Paul Hanson and Patrick Borelli
Photo editors: Aaron Clendening and Lindsay Blatt
Special thanks to Susan Bolotin, Ellen Lewis,
Randall Lotowycz, and Richard Lingeman

Workman books are available at special discounts
when purchased in bulk for premiums and sales
promotions as well as for fund-raising or educational
use. Special editions or book excerpts can also be
created to specification. For details, contact the
Special Sales Director at the address below.

Workman Publishing Company, Inc.
225 Varick Street
New York, NY 10014-4381
www.workman.com

Printed in the United States of America
First printing September 2006

10 9 8 7 6 5 4 3 2 1

To George Mason, Thomas
Jefferson, James Madison,
Abraham Lincoln, and
Franklin Delano Roosevelt

INTRODUCTION

Most political humor is a form of reasoned argument, but with all the supporting evidence left out. What remains is the joke--and those who get it are expected to already know the critique that prompted the gag in the first place.

In this book, we're not taking any chances. We've put the evidence back in; on roughly every fourth page, we present a "Sad Truth" about George W. Bush's presidency,

a factual reminder of the painful realities that made this book possible. Think of the Sad Truths as a brief refresher course on the Bush Years. The photo captions are entirely made up; the Sad Truths are entirely not. The sources for them--reputable news organizations, research entities, government records, and court decisions--are listed in the back.

We don't think that George Bush's presidency is a laughing matter. That's why we've written a humor book about it. Sure, time eventually stops the spin, rubs off the makeup, and reveals men and women in power for what they are, and were; but in a democracy, this is a poor consolation prize. Our hope is that we might soon look back on this maddening time and laugh at jokes that aren't on us.

R. D. Rosen
Harry Prichett
Rob Battles

"Can you believe it? I really
am the president!"

"Wait, here's the awesome part,
Tony: I totally convinced
Congress that our Constitution
allows it!"

The sad Truth

President George W. Bush has made unprecedented claims of executive power. He has asserted, for example, that the president may imprison foreign nationals and American citizens without judicial process and may hold such persons incommunicado. In rejecting these claims in 2004, Justice Sandra Day O'Connor wrote for the Supreme Court, "History and common sense teach us that an unchecked system of detention carries the potential to become a means for oppression."

BAD PRESIDENT
WARNING SIGN #307

First lady sometimes helps
president form words in
English.

"Listen, you pain in the ass--
just ask the damn questions
on the printout."

"Don't give me the actual
numbers, you knucklehead.
Give me *our* numbers."

The **sad** Truth

In the months before the invasion of Iraq, General Eric Shinseki, the army chief of staff, told Secretary of Defense Donald Rumsfeld that 300,000 to 400,000 troops would be necessary to bring about a stable Iraq. Rumsfeld, who had no personal experience with ground war, dismissed Shinseki's estimate as "far off the mark." Rumsfeld insisted that 140,000 troops could accomplish the mission. Four years later, despite sectarian violence, lethal attacks on American troops, and mass murders, American troop levels are less than 150,000, a figure called insufficient by, among many others, General Anthony Zinni, former Centcom commander; Colonel John Agoglia, planner for Centcom; and Senator John McCain.

Deputy Chiefs of Staff Joseph
Hagin and Karl Rove consult
secret Republican diet plan
to stay overweight and pasty
at taxpayers' expense.

"My acid reflux disappeared
the minute I stopped worrying
about reality."

Vice President Cheney attends
ground-breaking ceremony
for new Museum of Modern
American Torture.

The sad Truth

On September 16, 2001, Vice President Dick Cheney said on *Meet the Press,* "We have to work, though, sort of the dark side. . . . A lot of what needs to be done here will have to be done quietly, without any discussion."

On June 29, 2006, in *Hamdan v. Rumsfeld,* which dealt with military tribunals, the United States Supreme Court held that for the past five years the Bush administration's treatment of terrorist suspects had been in violation of American law, U.S. military law, and—according to Justice John Stevens's Opinion of the Court—Common Article 3 of the Geneva Conventions. That article forbids "outrages upon [the] personal dignity" of wartime prisoners as well as "humiliating and degrading treatment," such as the abuses that occurred at Abu Ghraib prison under the jurisdiction of Secretary of Defense Donald Rumsfeld.

On August 9, 2006, six weeks after *Hamdan v. Rumsfeld,* the *Washington Post* reported that the administration had drafted amendments to the U.S. War Crimes Act that would grant immunity from criminal prosecution to political appointees, CIA officers, and former members of the military who had violated portions of Common Article 3.

11

"Buchanan, Andrew Johnson,
and that guy who invented the
vacuum cleaner--right off the
bat, that's three presidents
worse than me."

"That's funny--he said the WMDs were right next to the socket wrenches."

BAD PRESIDENT
EARLY WARNING SIGN #200

Presidential candidate shows
schoolchildren how to cover
ears to block out other
people's opinions.

The **sad** Truth

In 2001 Richard Clarke, the government's senior counterterrorism expert when Bush took office, urged the administration to get more aggressive with al Qaeda, which he viewed as the primary threat to American security. Bush's national security advisor Condoleezza Rice responded by downgrading his status and refusing to let him speak directly to the president or secretary of defense. Clarke resigned in 2003.

When General Eric Shinseki, four-star army chief of staff, told the president he should double the number of troops in Iraq, Rumsfeld appointed the general's successor an unprecedented 14 months before the end of Shinseki's term. Equally unprecedented, at Shinseki's resignation ceremony, customarily attended by the secretary of defense, no senior administration official was present.

BAD PRESIDENT
EARLY WARNING SIGN #418

Future president lobbies
Texas Air National Guard for
cup holders in all aircraft.

"For me, all truths are inconvenient."

BAD PRESIDENT
WARNING SIGN #429

President answers questions about newly decorated White House Welcome Center.

The sad Truth

During the run-up to his first presidential campaign, President Bush told Texas evangelist James Robinson, "I feel like God wants me to run for president. I can't explain it, but I sense my country is going to need me. Something is going to happen. I know it won't be easy for me or my family, but God wants me to do it."

"Maybe this gay marriage thing isn't so bad after all."

President tells Caucasian
Coalition how much time
he spends thinking about
minorities.

"Are the Levees Jewish?"

The sad Truth

On September 1, 2005, two days after Hurricane Katrina hit New Orleans, President Bush announced on *Good Morning America,* "I don't think anybody anticipated the breach of the levees."

In fact, on the day *before* Katrina hit New Orleans, federal disaster officials had warned the president specifically about the levees in a videotaped meeting, later obtained by the Associated Press. In addition, the National Hurricane Center, FEMA, and other federal agencies had been tracking and assessing the gigantic storm during the week before the Louisiana landfall.

*"Même quand je parle anglais,
il ne comprend rien."*

("Even when I speak English, he
doesn't understand anything.")

BAD PRESIDENT
WARNING SIGN #11

At Constitution Ball, no one
notices that president and
first lady have been replaced
by animatronic versions of
themselves.

Secretary of State Colin
Powell holds up classified
photo of WMDs for reporters.

The sad Truth

After privately questioning for months the wisdom of invading Iraq, Secretary of State Colin Powell went before the United Nations General Assembly in February 2003 to make the case for a UN resolution authorizing such an invasion. The speech was an important declaration of the administration's position, especially considering Powell's great credibility with the American public. Powell stated unequivocally that Iraq already possessed chemical and biological weapons and was actively developing nuclear weapons. In doing so, Powell was relying on intelligence provided by CIA director George Tenet and other intelligence officials, who had, as it turned out, been pressured by Vice President Cheney and Secretary Rumsfeld to present as established facts information that the intelligence officials themselves thought questionable.

"Wonderful! Joe and Valerie won't know what hit them."

CIA director George Tenet
scolds FBI director Robert
Mueller for bugging him about
sharing secrets.

"Wolfowitz wants to know if you're still mad at him for the Iraq thing."

The sad Truth

As deputy secretary of defense, Paul Wolfowitz was an architect and ardent supporter of the invasion of Iraq, claiming that Americans would be regarded as liberators and as the founders of the first Arab democracy. He told Congress the war would pay for itself with Iraqi oil. Nevertheless, President Bush appointed Wolfowitz president of the World Bank in 2005, the same job LBJ gave Robert McNamara in 1968 after he served as secretary of defense during the Vietnam War.

Bush explains that his head should be slightly bigger than the others on Mount Rushmore.

"Are you two touching
yourselves? I'm touching
myself."

"And you say the homeless are actually hungry enough to eat this crap?"

The sad Truth

The poverty rate in the United States has risen each year of President Bush's administration: 12.7 percent of Americans are now living in poverty. Between 2001 and 2004, poverty among African-Americans rose from 22.7 to 24.7 percent. Child poverty rose from 16.3 percent in 2001 to 17.8 percent in 2004. Between 1999 and 2004, median household income dropped 5.9 percent.

"Welcome to our side, Joe.
Your new Republican name
is Biff Lane III."

"Don't worry--it'll all be over
in a couple of years."

"I *am* smiling, goddammit!"

The sad Truth

During Vice President Cheney's tenure as CEO of Halliburton (1995–2000), the company had substantial interests in two firms that sold more than $73 million of oil production equipment to Saddam Hussein's Iraq. In September 1998 Cheney oversaw Halliburton's acquisition of Dresser Industries Inc., which sold pumps, spare parts, and pipeline equipment to Iraq through two subsidiaries (of which Halliburton later divested itself, in 1999). Although the subsidiaries made sales to Iraq of $30 million during his tenure, Cheney claims he was unaware that the corporations were doing business with Iraq. Upon leaving Halliburton in 2000, Vice President Cheney received stock options of 433,333 shares of the company (worth about $13 million in September 2006).

Halliburton and its subsidiary KBR have received substantial noncompetitive contracts for the rebuilding of Iraq and have been the subject of U.S. Army investigations regarding the costs of their work.

"Barney, I'm not at liberty to
discuss that at this time.
Next question. Yes, Barney?"

"Speak up. I like a man with ideas."

"Madame Secretary, when you're
through with that body armor,
can I have it for my men?"

The sad Truth

O n December 8, 2004, at a base in Kuwait, Army Specialist Thomas Wilson of the Tennessee National Guard 278th Regimental Combat Team asked Secretary Rumsfeld, "Why do we soldiers have to dig through local landfills for pieces of scrap metal and compromised ballistic glass to up-armor our vehicles?"

"A s you know," Rumsfeld responded, "you go to war with the army you have. They're not the army you might want or wish to have at a later time."

"You're being silly, George.
Your biceps are every bit as
big as Rummy's."

"This is great! I'm *in* Senegal and I have *no* idea where Senegal is."

"Son, I see you're getting the hang of convincing the middle class we actually care about them."

The sad Truth

In 2006 the president's tax policy resulted in an average tax benefit of $23 for Americans in the lowest 20 percent of personal income. The middle 20 percent of Americans received a benefit of $748. The top 1 percent of Americans received an average tax benefit of $39,000. Individuals making more than $10 million a year saw their tax bill decrease by an average of $500,000.

"And get this, Donald--
I'm using our tax refund
to buy Hummers for all
the grandkids."

President Bush makes South Korean president cry by telling him North Korea thinks he's a wuss.

"Because this part of my
prefrontal cortex did not
develop normally, I have
trouble anticipating the
consequences of my actions."

The **sad** Truth

At an April 13, 2004, press conference, a member of the White House press corps asked the president to name a mistake he had made in office. "I wish you would have given me this written question ahead of time, so I could plan for it," he replied. "I'm sure something will pop into my head here in the midst of this press conference, with all the pressure of trying to come up with an answer, but it hadn't yet." Appearing confused, the president added, "I don't want to sound like I have made no mistakes. I'm confidant I have." He then went on to say: "Maybe I'm not as quick on my feet as I should be in coming up with one."

BAD PRESIDENT
WARNING SIGN #837

President poses as waiter at
diplomatic function in order to
avoid boring conversations with
Chinese officials about trade.

House majority leader Tom DeLay signals victory in bitterly fought competition for Most Corrupt Man in American Politics.

"This is where Dick and I do naughty things to ordinary Americans."

The sad Truth

In early 2002 President Bush issued a secret executive order authorizing the National Security Agency to engage in electronic eavesdropping, without judicial warrant, on phone calls between Americans and foreign nationals. The president's action was of dubious legality—he had failed to abide by the Foreign Intelligence Surveillance Act of 1978, which provides a court to oversee government domestic spying in the name of national security. The Supreme Court has yet to rule.

It suddenly dawns on first lady what she's gotten herself into.

"I can bore anyone. It's a gift."

Vice President Cheney helps
begin countdown to end of
president's workday.

The sad Truth

President Bush originally opposed the establishment of the 9/11 Commission, a bipartisan body charged with investigating the September 11 attacks and the American government's failure to prevent them. After weeks of negotiation with the commission, the president reluctantly agreed to an informal meeting at the White House, provided the vice president could go with him. The president was not under oath and no transcript of the discussion was made.

"Good news. I've narrowed down my search for a new secretary of education."

Deputy Secretary of Defense
Paul Wolfowitz plays the role
of "brave fighter pilot" in
the White House production
of *Mission Accomplished:
The Musical.*

Child informs president he was left behind.

The **sad** Truth

A 2005 report by the bipartisan National Council of State Legislatures strongly criticized the Bush administration's No Child Left Behind educational program, noting that the administration had funded only 8 percent of local school budgets, while requiring changes in nearly *every* public school's entire curriculum. One change was mandatory testing of students to measure school performance and maintain eligibility for continued federal funding. The mandatory tests have had the unintended consequence of diverting teachers' energy from educating children to administrative duties such as appraising the appraisals of multiple versions of mandatory tests.

President explains to a
gathering of Christian
fundamentalists the best
way to identify Jewish
people.

"Okay, that's not nice, guys.
I don't make fun of your
intelligence."

"Can I count on your support,
then?"

The sad Truth

In January 2006 NASA's top climate expert, James Hansen, said the Bush administration had forbidden him to speak publicly about global warming and the need to reduce greenhouse gases. The following month, Dr. Donald Kennedy, editor-in-chief of *Science* magazine, reported that the National Oceanic and Atmospheric Administration had ordered its scientists not to give interviews about a study linking ocean warming to increased hurricane intensity.

These acts of censorship corroborated a 2004 report from the Union of Concerned Scientists that charged President Bush with promoting ideology over good science when appointing governmental panels investigating global warming, air pollution, public health, and basic scientific research. The report was endorsed by 8,000 American scientists, 49 Nobel Laureates, and 63 winners of the national Medal of Science.

Karl Rove welcomes lobbyists to opening of new discount beverage and scam center in suburban Virginia.

Queen of Jordan and first
lady attend fund-raiser
with head of CIA Undercover
Operations and his wife.

BAD PRESIDENT
EARLY WARNING SIGN #34

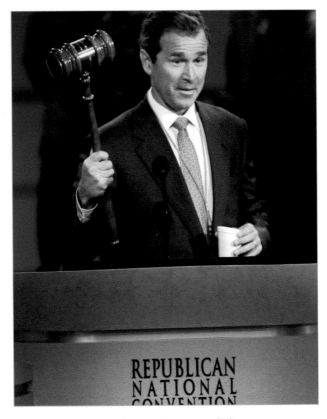

Governor tries to sell
Republicans on cheaper way
to execute Texas death row
prisoners.

The sad Truth

As Governor of Texas, Bush presided over 152 executions, by far the most of any contemporary governor. In 2003 journalist Alan Berlow asked Alberto R. Gonzalez, who was then special presidential counsel, whether Bush, as Texas governor, had read the clemency petitions that he regularly denied. "From time to time," the future attorney general replied.

Turkey thanks president for
Thanksgiving pardon.

President answers a question about his latest foreign policy initiative.

"No, sir, not that one. Over there is the Fox reporter."

The **sad** Truth

Fox News Channel CEO Roger Ailes, who once served as media advisor to President Nixon and also served in the Reagan and George H. W. Bush administrations, sent a note in 2002 to George Bush advisor Karl Rove suggesting how the administration might maintain public support for its policies. The channel's own support for the administration's policies was evident when, on March 23, 2003, Fox News reported a "huge chemical weapons factory found in southern Iraq." Just three weeks later, Fox News reported "weapons-grade plutonium possibly found at Iraq nuclear complex." Neither the factory nor the complex actually existed.

A year-long University of Maryland study found that viewers of Fox News—the most watched 24-hour cable news channel—were more likely than other Americans to believe misinformation about the Iraq War.

"I love this time of day,
when the sun's going down
and you can hear the sound
of Mexicans crossing the
border."

President unveils new "Patriot Shoe," which all Americans will have to wear by fall 2007, or be deported.

BAD PRESIDENT
WARNING SIGN #439

In effort to boost plummeting
approval ratings among
minorities, president rubs
lucky black man's head.

The **sad** Truth

In the 2004 presidential election, only 25 percent of black Americans voted. Of those who voted, 11 percent voted for President Bush.

BAD PRESIDENT
WARNING SIGN #308

Milwaukee manager Davey Lopes
gently leads president to
dugout after Bush enters
trance and tries to pitch
entire inning against
Cincinnati.

BAD PRESIDENT
EARLY WARNING SIGN #441

Candidate uses illegal
blocking maneuver to keep
Democratic voters away from
Florida polling places.

"*This* is the natural resource
we need to protect: aging, rich
white men in cowboy hats."

The sad Truth

During President Bush's stewardship of the environment, toxic waste cleanups fell 52 percent. Criminal prosecutions of polluters dropped 17 percent. Beach closings rose 26 percent.

CIA's George Tenet prepares to blow lunch in response to yet another question about 9/11.

President and first lady wonder why $14 billion antiflood device didn't protect New Orleans.

Deputy Secretary of Defense
Paul Wolfowitz grows wistful
for the days when the
administration could do
anything it wanted to Abu
Ghraib detainees.

The sad Truth

Forty American soldiers have been criminally prosecuted for abuse of detainees at Abu Ghraib prison. Only three of the 40 have been officers, and even in these cases the doctrine of command responsibility was not an issue. More than two years after the Abu Ghraib scandal broke, no senior commander or civilian superior in the chain of command has faced criminal charges for systematic abuse and torture at the prison.

One of the two civilians in the chain of command, Secretary of Defense Rumsfeld (the other one being President Bush), once asked why detainees could be forced to stand for *only* four hours a day, joking that he himself often stood "for eight to ten hours a day." "Torture?" he exclaimed. "That's not torture!"

President makes Dick Cheney's lesbian daughter wear disguise at White House functions.

President reprimands Lyudmila
Putin for speaking a foreign
language in the White House.

"Remind me, Dick. Which ones are the Axis of Evil?"

The sad Truth

In his 2002 State of the Union address, President Bush declared Iraq, Iran, and North Korea an "Axis of Evil." Two of these countries, Iran and North Korea, were, and are, actively developing nuclear weapons. President Bush attacked the third.

BAD PRESIDENT
WARNING SIGN #75

President and first lady
honor children tricked by
White House into playing
embryos in holiday anti-
stem cell pageant.

"Mr. President, guess who's not wearing underpants?"

BAD PRESIDENT
EARLY WARNING SIGN #7

Future president's father
ecstatic when son receives
U.S. Air Force's Showing Up
from Time to Time Award.

The sad Truth

George Bush joined the Texas Air National Guard, where he was trained as an F-102 pilot. After winning his wings, he transferred to the guard's "Champagne unit," made up of the sons of privileged Texas families who wanted to avoid serving in Vietnam. During his six-year period of obligation, Bush was absent for months at a time, without leave or explanation.

The air force suspended his flight status 18 months before his enlistment elapsed. He received an honorable discharge six months early, without further official comment.

FEMA director Michael Brown surveys the damage to his career.

"I'm sorry. Could you ask me
something else?"

President celebrates passage
of bill prohibiting birthday
cake desecration.

The **sad** Truth

In summer 2003 President Bush endorsed amending the First Amendment to make desecration of the American flag unconstitutional. (Although the proposal died in the Senate, the issue did succeed in putting the Kerry/Edwards ticket on the defensive in 2004.) Fourteen years earlier in *Texas v. Johnson,* the United States Supreme Court had held unconstitutional a Texas statute prohibiting flag desecration. In his Opinion of the Court, Justice William J. Brennan wrote: "We do not consecrate the flag by punishing its desecration, for in doing so we dilute the freedom that this cherished emblem represents."

"Hello, Iraqi freedom lovers!
Let the democracy begin!"

President threatens to hold breath until Liechtenstein joins the Coalition of the Willing.

Karl Rove throws temper tantrum and won't let *Air Force One* take off until president gives him window seat.

The sad Truth

On June 22, 2005, while addressing the Conservative Party of New York State, Karl Rove said, "Conservatives saw the savagery of 9/11 and the attacks and prepared for war; liberals saw the savagery of the 9/11 attacks and wanted to prepare indictments and offer therapy and understanding for our attackers."

Families of September 11, an organization of those who lost relatives in the attacks, asked Rove to "stop trying to reap political gain in the tragic misfortune of others" and called his behavior "offensive."

The sad Truth

On April 8, 2004, then–
National Security Advisor
Condoleezza Rice testified
before the 9/11 Commission
that there was "nothing that
suggested there was going to
be a threat to the United States"
in the Presidential Daily Briefing
Document on August 6, 2001.
However, Rice proceeded to
admit that the title of the
document was "Bin Laden
Determined to Attack Inside
the United States."

President tries on new pair of designer blinders.

"Very funny, Ted. Now pull 'em
up and get outta here!"

"And then I told 'em it was an orange alert--and, by God, they fell for it!"

The sad Truth

Among the many career army officers who are not impressed by Secretary of Defense Rumsfeld's aggressive, can-do public persona is Lieutenant General David McKiernan, who commanded all U.S. ground troops in Iraq from 2002 to 2004. "In lieu of an order . . . or plan," McKiernan has said, "you get a set of PowerPoint slides." "To imagine that PowerPoint slides can substitute for [formal written orders]," said Colonel Andrew Bacevich, commander of an armored cavalry regiment, "is really the height of recklessness." Military correspondent Thomas Ricks of the *Washington Post* likened Rumsfeld's approach to being a garage mechanic who uses a glossy sales brochure to figure out how to fix a car.

"It's funny, Bill. I'm beginning
to think my Dick is more
dangerous than yours."

"Hmmm . . . that's an interesting point. I think I'll ignore it."

"Nice to see you, son. I'm a big fan of the Dunkin' Donuts Whopper."

The **sad** Truth

President Bush's budget for fiscal year 2007 called for a cut of $108 million in the Federal Supplemental Food Program for the poor, reducing food subsidies for 420,000 elderly Americans and 50,000 pregnant women. This policy will put recipients at greater risk for poor nutrition and resulting health problems; scientific research suggests that in poor neighborhoods, both supermarkets and fast-foods outlets are less likely to stock and sell nutritious food than they are in more affluent ones.

Pentagon shows Bush new
$1.2 million flashlight.

The sad Truth

President Bush has proposed a record defense budget of $439 billion for fiscal year 2007. This budget does not include funding of the wars in Iraq and Afghanistan (another $252 billion), which are dealt with through supplemental appropriations bills. By the end of September 2006, the military cost of the Iraq War will have been $182 billion, with a projected future annual cost of $80–100 billion a year.

Bush tries to explain to the
queen of England and the
duke of Edinburgh why he's
wearing women's shoes.

President continues to be at a loss over what to do.

"It's the president, General. Remember, speak slowly and enunciate."

The sad Truth

In April 2006 six retired army and marine corps generals, including two who were ground commanders in Iraq, called for the resignation of Secretary of Defense Rumsfeld, citing his hostility to the uniformed military and his incompetent planning for the war in, and occupation of, Iraq. In a written White House response, President Bush replied that the secretary had the president's "full support and deepest appreciation."

"You sure know a lot about geography, Vladimir."

The sad Truth

In December 2001 CIA paramilitary units and U.S special forces had Osama bin Laden trapped at a site in the Tora Bora mountains of Afghanistan, leaving him an escape route only through the snow-covered mountains to Pakistan. When the CIA leader of the operation requested one battalion of U.S. Army Rangers to block bin Laden's path, General Tommy Franks, commander of United States Central Command, refused, saying that "the Afghans themselves wanted to get into Tora Bora," and he didn't want to introduce "non-Afghan troops at that time." Bin Laden escaped.

"I'm so tired of trying to
appear intelligent."

"Oh, boy. I hope somebody's writing this down."

"Remind me to invade every country that doesn't speak English."

The sad Truth

When the nonpartisan Pew Global Attitudes Project asked citizens of 16 nations in Europe, the Middle East, and Asia in June 2005 to give favorability ratings for five major nations—the United States, Germany, China, Japan, and France—the United States came in last. Among those surveyed, a low regard for President Bush more heavily correlated with an unfavorable view of the United States than any other factor. Interestingly, Americans harbor few illusions about their country's reputation abroad. Almost seven out of ten persons— 69 percent—believe the United States is "generally disliked abroad."

The president reassures elderly
voters that the repeal of the
death tax will be retroactive.

"I love tuna!"

BAD PRESIDENT
WARNING SIGN #622

President determines what is,
and what is not, brush.

The sad Truth

By August 2006, halfway through his second term, President Bush had spent 370 days—more than a year—at his Crawford, Texas, ranch. (This figure does not include time spent at the family estate in Kennebunkport, Maine, or the presidential retreat at Camp David.) He didn't interrupt his Texas vacations until early in his second term. He flew to Washington in March 2005 to sign a bill overturning a Florida court order that granted Terri Schiavo's husband's request to cut off the severely brain-damaged woman's life support. The White House acknowledged that the president could have signed the bill in Texas.

BAD PRESIDENT
WARNING SIGN #50

President reenacts his 1976
DUI arrest for visiting
dignitaries.

"There's never any bourbon at these damn liberation parties."

President unveils design for
new American flag.

The **sad** Truth

On August 1, 2005, during a White House session with Texas newspaper reporters, the president remarked that intelligent design—the idea that the universe must have been authored by a higher being—should be taught in the public schools along with evolution. The president's statement did not surprise Bruce Alberts, president of the National Academy of Sciences, who had previously warned colleagues in a public letter of "increasingly strident attempts to limit the teaching of evolution." In response to attacks on evolution, the National Academy of Sciences has created a website specifically to counter antievolutionist claims.

"Two things: Don't go in there for a while, and don't let 'em serve me any more goat."

"Hand me the remote. This
Katrina stuff is bumming
me out."

"You're sure I can't interest
you in a deferment, young
lady?"

The sad Truth

Two years after September 11, 2001, and even though the American intelligence community had found no credible evidence to support the idea that Saddam Hussein was involved in the terrorist attacks, Vice President Cheney continued to make the claim. On NBC's *Meet the Press* on November 14, 2003, the vice president asserted that the administration was "learning more and more" about connections between Iraq and al Qaeda "before 9/11."

Former CIA counterterrorism expert Vincent Cannistraro, who served as director of intelligence programs at the National Security Council under Reagan, was quoted in the *Boston Globe* as saying that Cheney's "willingness to use speculation and conjecture as facts in public presentations is appalling."

BAD PRESIDENT
WARNING SIGN #194

President's father prefers
philandering Democratic
ex-president to own offspring
who screwed entire country.

"... God, I wish I could just get hammered ..."

BAD PRESIDENT
WARNING SIGN #83

President always last to be
called on by UN Security
Council.

The sad Truth

On March 7, 2005, President Bush nominated former Undersecretary of State for Arms Control John Bolton to be United States ambassador to the UN, even though Bolton had previously observed, "If the UN secretary [sic] building in New York lost ten stories, it wouldn't make a bit of difference." After Senators Chafee (R-R.I.) and Voinovich (R-Ohio) of the Senate Foreign Relations Committee raised questions concerning his temperament and mistreatment of subordinates—and after a former head of state department intelligence, Carl W. Ford, called Bolton "a quintessential kiss-up, kick-down sort of guy"—his nomination stalled in the Senate. He is the UN ambassador by virtue of a presidential recess appointment that will remain in effect until Congress reconvenes in 2007.

Secretary of Defense Rumsfeld
leads new Iraqi war recruits
in prayer.

BAD PRESIDENT
WARNING SIGN #408

President's mother checks son's
breath before he meets with
Joint Chiefs of Staff.

"George Tenet, General Franks, Paul Bremer--it's rare for me to honor even *one* person more inept than me, let alone three."

The **sad** Truth

Two weeks prior to President Bush's decision to invade Iraq, George Tenet, director of the CIA, famously told the president that the case for nuclear weapons in Iraq was a "slam dunk." He resigned on June 3, 2004.

Centcom commander General Tommy Franks was responsible for the invasion and occupation of Iraq, but showed little interest in Iraq's postwar stability. Official U.S. Army historian Major Isaiah Wilson III concluded that Franks had no plan for the occupation of Iraq, all but insuring an insurgency and sectarian violence. General Franks resigned on July 7, 2003.

On May 23, 2003, Paul Bremer, head of the Coalition Provisional Authority in Iraq, ordered the dissolution of the Iraqi army, domestic security services, and police—without consulting Washington. The decision put 720,000 Iraqi men out of work, instantly creating disorder, resentment, and an ample source of manpower for the insurgency and sectarian militias. Bremer resigned on June 28, 2004.

On December 14, 2004, President Bush awarded Tenet, Franks, and Bremer each the Medal of Freedom, the highest civilian honor an American can receive.

"Gee, Dick, I don't know--
bombing Massachusetts is a
tough sell."

"Wow, that was great! I only
wish the border was longer."

"Let me finish my lunch and
I'll lie to you some more about
the war on terrorism."

The sad Truth

Following the invasion of Iraq, a number of reporters and commentators raised the question of why the press had been so uncritical of administration claims and justifications for going to war. Christiane Amanpour, CNN's well-known chief foreign correspondent, stated the press was "intimidated." "I think the press was self-muzzled. I'm sorry to say that television, and perhaps, to a certain extent, my station was intimidated by the administration and its foot soldiers at Fox News."

Nor were media regrets limited to television. On May 26, 2004, the *New York Times* published a mea culpa from the editors for printing numerous untrue articles suggesting that Saddam Hussein was actively developing nuclear weapons and possessed biological and chemical weapons—articles that "depended at least in part on information from . . . Iraqi informants, defectors, and exiles . . . whose credibility has come under increasing public debate in recent weeks." The *Times* concluded that the blame for misreporting fell upon "editors at several levels," who should have pressed for more skepticism, but were "perhaps too intent on rushing scoops."

BAD PRESIDENT
WARNING SIGN #73

Following Katrina, President
Bush requires FEMA officials
to appear incognito at all
press conferences.

President completes memoirs.

"Go away. Leave me alone. Get your own deficit numbers."

The sad Truth

In his first year in office President Bush turned the $127 billion budget surplus he inherited from President Clinton into a deficit. When Secretary of the Treasury Paul O'Neill told Vice President Cheney after the 2002 midterm elections that a second round of Bush tax cuts would be irresponsible, given the costs of 9/11 and the war in Afghanistan (the invasion of Iraq was still a year away), the vice president replied, "You know, Paul, Reagan proved deficits don't matter. We won the midterm elections. This is our due."

O'Neill was fired before the end of the year. The current national debt is $8.4 trillion, compared to $5.7 trillion in the last year of the Clinton administration.

"I wish I could quit you,
Karl."

BAD PRESIDENT
WARNING SIGN #71

President keeps asking world leaders how much time he has left as U.S. president.

BAD PRESIDENT
WARNING SIGN #35

President amuses staff with impression of elderly man befuddled by Medicare prescription drug program.

The sad Truth

President Bush's Medicare Part D Prescription Drug Program, the biggest change in Medicare in 40 years, was intended to provide "flexibility" in meeting the prescription needs of the elderly. Unfortunately, only about one in six eligible seniors has signed up for the program. The reason seems to be incurable confusion. A senior citizen must choose from a variety of insurance plans, including some that do not yet exist, and the plans may limit coverage to certain drugs and have different rates of co-payment. Low-income applicants must fill out a four-page form in addition to the normal application. Administration officials cite language barriers as a partial explanation for the lack of public participation.

President Bush's proposed 2007 budget seeks to cut Medicare by $14 billion over five years.

BAD PRESIDENT
WARNING SIGN #84

White House officials laugh
at voters after president
fools them again.

Source Notes

The source (or sources) for each Sad Truth can be found in the citations below. For background, I relied upon a number of books concerning the war in Iraq, the Bush administration, and the problem of international terrorism. *Cobra II* by Michael R. Gordon and General Bernard E. Trainor (Pantheon, 2006) and *Fiasco* by Thomas E. Ricks (The Penguin Press, 2006) present superb analyses of the war. The former focuses upon American military operations on the ground and the surprises Americans faced there; the latter goes beyond the invasion to analyze both the fighting and the politics of the occupation and insurgency. Each book gives a remarkable account of the strained relationship between Secretary of Defense Rumsfeld and the United States Army. Taken together, the two books provide a portrait of how the Bush administration works, and doesn't, in time of war.

Fouad Adjami, professor of Middle East Studies at The School of Advanced International Studies at Johns Hopkins University, has written an excellent book, *The Foreigner's Gift* (Free Press, 2006), on the culture and politics of the Muslim world in Iraq and beyond. The book sheds light as well upon American power and naïveté in the Middle East. Richard A. Clarke's *Against All Enemies* (Free Press, 2004) is useful for understanding the administration responses to 9/11. Gary Berntsen and Ralph Pezzullo's *Jawbreaker* (Crown, 2005) gives the most detailed account to date of the American attempt to trap Bin Laden in Tora Bora in December 2001.

Other books on terrorism worth noting include *The Age of Sacred Terror* by Daniel Benjamin and Steven Simon (Random House, 2002), *Holy War Inc.* by Peter L. Bergen (Free Press, 2001), *Inside al Qaeda* by Rohan Gunaratna (Columbia University Press, 2002), and, of course, *The 9/11 Commission Report* (Norton, 2004). Seymour M. Hersh's *Chain of Command* (Harper Collins, 2004) and *The Abu Ghraib Investigations,* Steven Strasser, ed. (Public Affairs Reports, 2004) provide an understanding of the path to Abu Ghraib, as well as the specifics of the scandal itself.

Finally, for a deeper historical understanding of the Middle East, I recommend David Fromkin's *A Peace to End All Peace* (Henry Holt, 1989), which explains the origins of the modern Middle East following World War I and the region's resulting intractable problems. Peter Hopkirk's *The Great Game* (Kondasha America, 1994) provides similar historical insight for Afghanistan and Central Asia.

For matters of domestic policy, I relied upon the administration's budget priorities as outlined in each year's fiscal budget (Department of the Treasury) as well as mainstream press reports (CNN, the *New York Times,* the *Washington Post,* CBS News) of the administration's positions. Former Secretary of the Treasury Paul O'Neill's story, *The Price of Loyalty: George W. Bush, the White House and the Education of Paul O'Neill* by Ron Suskind (Simon & Shuster, 2004), offers something of a domestic analogue to Richard A. Clarke's picture of the administration's policy-making for terrorism.

—James Friedman

Pg. 3: *Hamdan v. Rumsfeld,* U.S. Supreme Court, 2006. *Hamdi v. Rumsfeld,* U.S. Supreme Court, 2004.

Pg. 7: *Cobra II,* Michael R. Gordon and General Bernard E. Trainor, Pantheon, NY, 2006. *Washington Post,* January 25, 2005. *Fiasco,* Thomas E. Ricks, Penguin Press, NY, 2006.

Pg. 11: *Hamdan v. Rumsfeld,* U.S. Supreme Court, 2006. PBS, *Frontline,* "The Dark Side," 2006.

Pg. 15: *Against All Enemies,* Richard A. Clarke, Free Press, NY, 2004. *Fiasco,* Ricks, supra.

Pg. 19: *The Faith of George W. Bush,* Stephen Mansfield, Tarcher, NY, 2003. *Observer,* November 2, 2003.

Pg. 23: Associated Press, March 1, 2006. *Washington Post,* March 1, 2006.

Pg. 27: *Fiasco,* Ricks, supra.

Pg. 31: *Fiasco,* Ricks, supra. *Washington Post,* March 17, 2005.

Pg. 35: U.S. Census Bureau, "Tables B-1 and B-2," August 2005. Americanprogress.org, "State of Presidential Credibility."

Pg. 39: CBS News, CBS.com, September 26, 2003. The Global Policy Forum

(globalpolicy.org/security/
sanction/iraq1/oilforfood/
2001/0627chen.htm).
Washington Post,
June 23, 2001.
Pg. 43: CNN.com,
December 9, 2004.
Washington Post,
December 15, 2004.
Pg. 47: Mobudget.org, "The
Missouri Budget Project
Report," February 2006.
Center for Budget and Policy,
Washington, DC
Pg. 51: Reuters,
April 14, 2004.
Pg. 55: *New York Times,*
December 16, 2005.
Pg. 59: CNN.com,
April 30, 2004.
BBC News, BBC.co.uk,
April 29, 2004.
Pg. 63: NCSL News,
February 23, 2005.
Choosing Excellence,
John Merrow, Scarecrow
Press, 2001.
San Francisco Chronicle,
"States Distort School
Tests, Researchers Say,"
June 30, 2006.
Pg. 67: NPR, *Weekend Edition,*
February 26, 2006.
Union of Concerned Scientists,
"Restoring Scientific Integrity
in Policy Making,"
February 18, 2004.
Pg. 71: Death Penalty
Information Center, 2004.

Atlantic, "The Texas Clemency
Memo," Alan Berlow,
July/August 2003.
Pg. 75: The Center for Media and
Democracy (Sourcewatch.org),
April 27, 2006.
Salon.com, March 30, 2004.
Pg. 79: Campusprogress.org,
July 13, 2006.
Pg. 83: Knight-Ridder
(commondreams.org/
headlines04/1013-12.htm),
"Environment Worsened
Under Bush in Many Key
Areas, Data Show,"
Seth Borenstein,
October 13, 2004.
Pg. 87: The Detainee Abuse and
Accountability Project (a joint
project of the New York
University Law School, Human
Rights First, and Human
Rights Watch), "Report,"
April 26, 2006.
Jurist, April 27, 2006.
New Yorker, "The Memo," Jane
Mayer, February 27, 2006.
Pg. 91: "State of the Union
Address," January 2002.
Pg. 95: *Air Force Times,*
September 27, 2004.
Pg. 99: *Texas v. Johnson,*
U.S. Supreme Court, 1989.
CBS News, CBS.com,
June 3, 2003.
Pg. 103: *Washington Post,*
June 24, 2005.
Mediamatters.org,
June 24, 2005.

Pg. 105: *New York Times,* "Text of Testimony of Condoleezza Rice before the 9/11 Commission," April 8, 2004.

Pg. 109: *Fiasco,* Ricks, supra.

Pg. 113: The Coalition for Human Needs, "Guide to FY Budget 2007." Centers for Disease Control, Department of Health and Human Services (www.cdc.gov), "The Roll of Race and Poverty in Access to Foods That Enable Individuals to Adhere to Dietary Guidelines," Elizabeth Baker, Mario Schootman, Ellen Barnidge, and Cheryl Kelly, July 5, 2006.

Pg. 115: NPR, August 2, 2006.

Pg. 119: CNN.com, April 14, 2006.

Pg. 121: *Jawbreaker,* Gary Bernsten and Ralph Pezzullo, Crown, NY, 2005.

Pg. 125: Pew Research Center, "Pew Global Attitudes Project," June 24, 2005.

Pg. 129: *Washington Post,* August 3, 2005. *New York Times,* March 21, 2005.

Pg. 133: *Washington Post,* August 3, 2005.

Pg. 137: *Boston Globe,* September 16, 2003.

Pg. 141: CNN.com, March 8, 2005. USAtoday.com, April 12, 2005.

Pg. 145: CNN.com, June 4, 2004. *Washington Post,* December 25, 2004. *Cobra II,* Gordon and Trainor, supra. *Fiasco,* Ricks, supra.

Pg. 149: *Editor and Publisher,* May 26, 2004. *New York Times,* May 26, 2004. *USA Today* (USAtoday.com), September 14, 2003.

Pg. 153: CBS, *Sixty Minutes,* January 11, 2004. U.S. Department of the Treasury (www.publicdebt.treas.gov).

Pg. 157: The Coalition for Human Needs, "Guide to FY Budget 2007." Slate.com, January 18, 2006. *Washington Post,* February 21, 2006. USAtoday.com, July 24, 2005.

Photo Credits

About the Authors

R. D. ROSEN once upon a time coined the word "psychobabble." He has written numerous books, including the forthcoming *A Buffalo in the House: The True Story of a Man, an Animal, and the American West,* to be published in Spring 2007.

HARRY PRICHETT has written and performed for the improv comedy group Chicago City Limits, created the off-off-Broadway one-man show *Work=Pain=Success,* and is the voice you hear on numerous television and radio commercials.

ROB BATTLES, who has written and produced for public radio stations and National Public Radio, is a senior vice president for a large, forward-looking media company.

Together, they wrote *Bad Baby, Bad Dog,* and (with Jim Edgar) *Bad Cat.*

JAMES FRIEDMAN, a professor of law at the University of Maine School of Law, specializes in constitutional law and counterterrorism. He has taught at the United States Military Academy at West Point and has been a visiting scholar at the Hebrew University in Jerusalem.